Business Intelligence

and how it can help you grow your business

Johan Faerch

Business Intelligence

Copyright © 2016 Johan Faerch

NPS Calculator is provided by Quicksearch Net Promoter® is a registered trademark of Satmetrix Systems, Inc., Bain & Company and Fred Reichheld.

All rights reserved.

ISBN: 9781794528802

Contents

What's in it for me?	4
Net Promoter Score (NPS)	7
Customer Profitability Score	10
Customer Profitability	13
Customer Conversion Rate	16
Customer Retention Rate	19
Customer Churn Rate	22
Customer Lifetime Period	25
Participants Registered	28
Registration by Type	31
Business Revenue	34
Group Revenue Rate	37
About the author	41

Business Intelligence

What's in it for me?

This book gives you a quick insight in some of the data you can use to improve your business. Data is an extremely powerful tool in your strategic work. If you dive into the examples with your own data you will quickly find areas where you can optimize your business and ultimately make more money.

This is not a comprehensive walk through of every KPI or possibility for using data nor is it meant to cover every detail in the examples. Instead it's meant to be a quick guide for you to get ideas for which data to look into in order to improve your business the most and give you 'the most bang for your buck'.

If nothing else is stated all examples and calculations are done per calendar year.

Please choose the areas most suited for you and just skip the rest for a starter.

Strategic Key Performance Indicators (KPIs)

Let's dive right in and get to work.

Top 5 do's

- Start with your business strategy
- Define the questions you need answers to
- Customize the KPIs to your needs
- Ensure that KPIs are owned and understood by people in your organization
- Use KPIs to improve performance

Start with the obvious: Your own business!

Make sure you have written down a clear strategy and from this define your own questions in order to start with the most relevant KPIs.

Top 5 don'ts

- Don't measure simply because other companies do
- Don't just measure what is easy to collect
- Don't let your KPIs get out of date
- Don't hard-wire your KPIs to incentive systems (ie bonuses)
- Don't use KPIs as a command and control tool

Data is a powerful tool when used correctly and equally dangerous when they are off heading, irrelevant or just plain wrong.

The first three bullet points are fairly easy to avoid – But please don't forget them!

The last two points basically mean that you shouldn't use your KPIs for anything but optimizing your business. Don't use them for neither hitting your staff on the head nor for rewarding them based on specific numbers.

Good luck

Business Intelligence

Do it yourself

My business strategy:

Questions I need answered:

My Key Performance Indicators:

This is how I will improve my business:

Business Intelligence

Net Promoter Score (NPS)

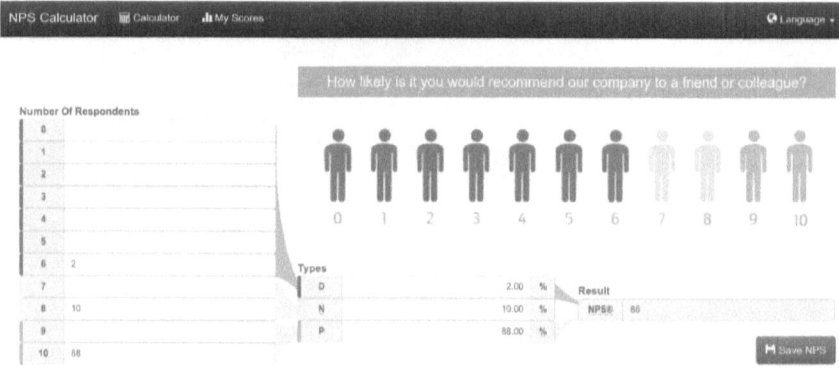

What is this?

This score is a very simple yet powerful measurement of what your customers think of your business. It's all the customer survey you need.

How do I find it?

You basically just ask your customers on a scale from 0 to 10: 'How likely is it you would recommend our company to a friend or a colleague?'

When you have the results go to the free website at http://npscalculator.com and punch in the numbers to get the final score.

How easy is it?

Setting up the survey and getting customers to answer is pretty hard but if you are willing to pay for it there are a lot of good consultants out there.

Finding the score is easy.

What is good?

Negative is BAD, 0-50 is GOOD, 50-100 is EXCELLENT.

What can I use it for?

Once you know your score you can use this as a benchmark for improving later surveys and you will know where to place your resources most efficiently, namely by first 'moving' 7s and 8s to become 9s and 10s.

Business Intelligence

Do it yourself

My Net Promoter Score:

I rate my NPS as:

I will work on this customer group:

I will improve my NPS by doing this:

Customer Profitability Score

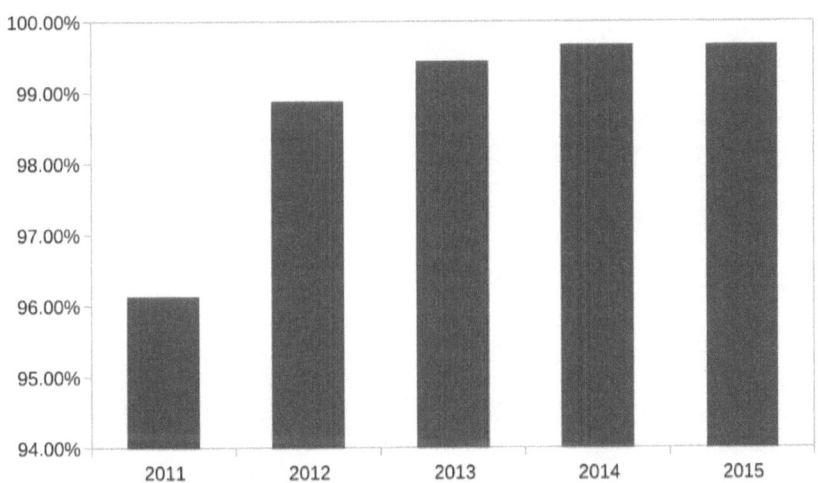

What is this?

The Customer Profitability Score is based on the revenue per customer with the direct marketing expenses per customer deducted. In the example it's measured per year over a period of five years.

Subjective notes on the example: "The figures are unusually high because the direct marketing expenses are very low. It's not viable to improve this further."

How do I find it?

Take your total revenue and divide by the number of customers you have (total revenue/number of customers). This gives you the revenue per customer.

Find the total of your direct marketing expenses in your accounting and divide by the number of customers you have (total direct marketing expenses/number of customers). This gives you the direct marketing expenses per customer.

To find the score in percent you then do: ((revenue per customer - direct marketing expenses per customer)/revenue per customer))*100

How easy is it?

Finding the numbers and the score is fairly easy.

What is good?

Higher values are good.

What can I use it for?

You get the facts concerning the efficiency of your expenses to acquire customers.

You can then work on lowering/optimizing your marketing expenses (and raising/optimizing your revenue).

Do it yourself

My revenue is:

My total number of customers is:

My total direct marketing expenses are:

My CPS is:

I rate my CPS as:

This is what I will do to improve my CPS:

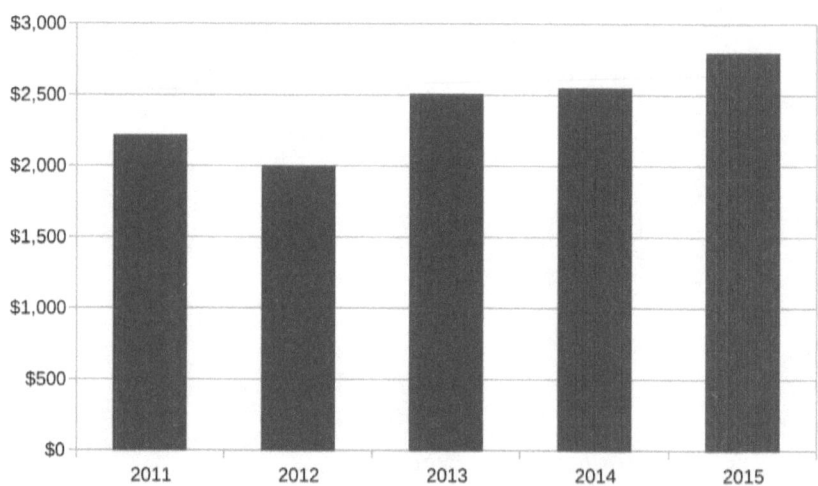

Customer Profitability

What is this?

The Customer Profitability is based on the revenue per customer with the direct marketing expenses per customer deducted. It's basically the same as the score just in Dollars instead of a percentage but as you see when you compare the two it shows you different information.

Subjective notes on the example: "The figures indicate room for improvement and are probably correlated with the low retention rate. The substantial and steady growth from 2012 to 2015 should be investigated further as the retention rate is almost fixed in this period. The 2012-2015 growth could be due to increased prices."

How do I find it?

You already have the numbers from the Customer Profitability Rate.

How easy is it?

Easy, as you already have the numbers from the Customer Profitability Rate.

What is good?

Higher values are good.

What can I use it for?

You get the facts concerning the value of a customer.

This can be further detailed by only calculating new customers and the price for aquiring these in order to see how long time it takes before you actually make a profit on a new customer.

You can then work on lowering/optimizing your marketing expenses and raising/optimizing your revenue.

Business Intelligence

Do it yourself

My Customer Profitability is:

I rate my CP as:

This is what I will do to improve my CP:

Customer Conversion Rate

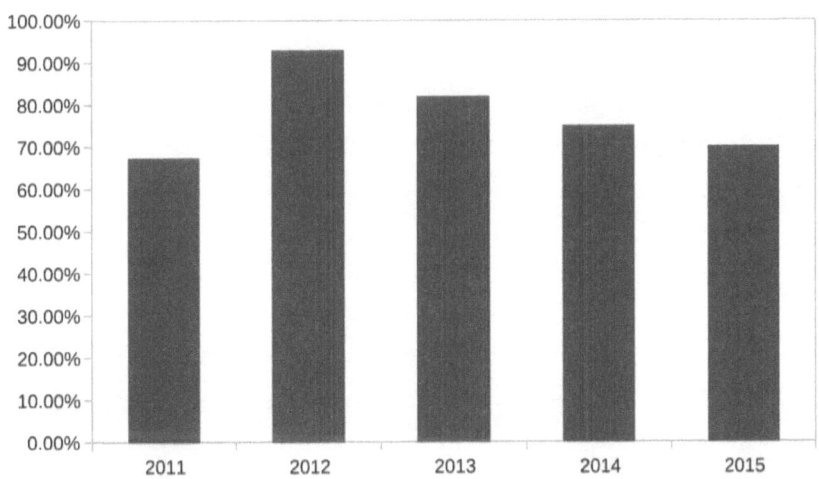

What is this?

The Customer Conversion Rate is based on the total number of new registered payers/members/persons any given year compared to the number that actually sign up for an activity.

Subjective notes on the example: "The conversion rate is relatively high but the decline 2012 to 2015 should be investigated."

How do I find it?

You find the total number of registered persons in your database and compare it to the total number of persons registered on an activity.

Remember the following

- You count unique persons and not individual registrations as one person might be registered multiple times.
- You only count the persons with member date the given year.

Both for new persons and registered customers.
- The list of persons registered is always included in the list of unique persons as they all have member date within the same year.
- If your business is dealing with families you calculate the entire family (the payer or the account) as one 'person'.

For an individual year do this: (Number of unique persons registered on activity / Total number of unique persons in database) * 100 = Customer Conversion Rate in percent.

How easy is it?

It should be fairly easy to draw the numbers from your database but it is crucial that you have the member-date/sign-up date registered.

What is good?

Higher values are good. But beware that the numbers are not high because you don't register non-buyers in your database!

What can I use it for?

The first thing you can use it for is to market your business directly to the list of persons who have not signed up.

Next you can try to identify the reasons why people are not signing up.

- Is it due to a lack of free slots in your activities?
- Is it due to a less than optimal administrative procedure?
- Is it due to people having difficulties signing up (obstacles in your on-boarding procedure)?
- Is it due to lack of information?

Business Intelligence

Do it yourself

My total number of new registered payers/members/persons is:

The number that actually sign up for an activity is:

My CCR is:

I rate my CCR as:

This is what I will do to improve my CCR:

Customer Retention Rate

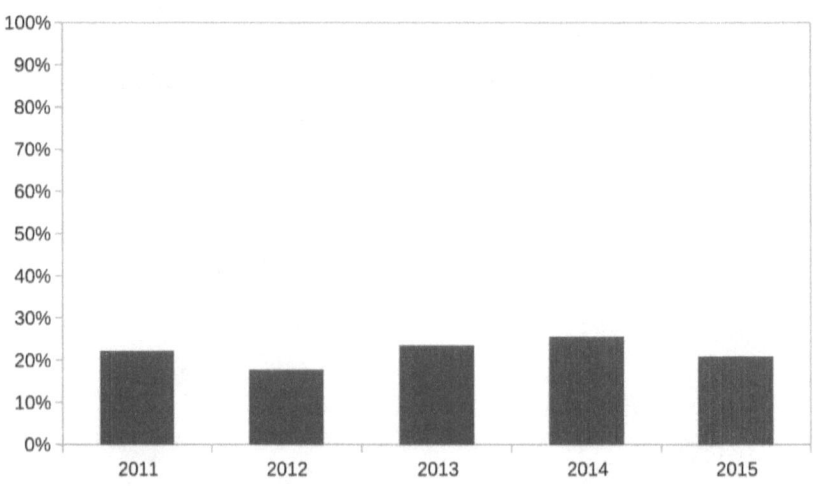

What is this?

The Customer Retention Rate shows you to what extent you are able to keep your customers.

This could be broken down to group level as some groups may have a significantly higher/lower retention rate compared to other groups.

The reciprocal value of this is the churn rate ie the percentage of customers lost which equals the customers worth win-back campaigning.

Subjective notes on the example: "The low retention rate should be investigated further and it might be interesting to look into the fact that the rate is more or less fixed even though the growth in registered participants is substantial."

How do I find it?

The percentage of participants during the given year who also participated on activities the preceding year: (unique participants this year who were also participants last year / unique participants last year) * 100 = Customer Retention Rate in percent.

How easy is it?

If you can deduct the numbers from your database it's easy. Otherwise it's pretty much impossible.

What is good?

Higher values are good.

What can I use it for?

This is a very strong tool for working on improving your business' ability to keep customers you have already acquired or just plain and simple getting more return business.

The first thing you can do is to directly approach the people who left your business.

Business Intelligence

Do it yourself

My total number of participants year 1 is:

My total number of participants year 2 is:

My CRR is:

I rate my CRR as:

This is what I will do to improve my CRR:

Customer Churn Rate

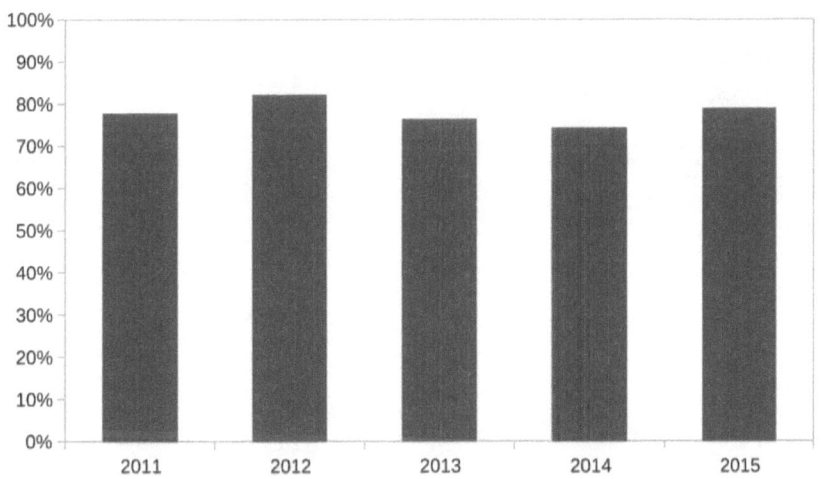

What is this?

The Churn Rate shows you to what extent your customers are leaving your business.

Subjective notes on the example: "This is a very high churn rate to any standards. The first investigation could look into the reason why customers are leaving."

How do I find it?

This is just the opposite of the Customer Retention Rate: 100% - Customer Retention Rate = Customer Churn Rate in percent.

How easy is it?

Once you have the Customer Retention Rate it is very easy.

What is good?

Lower values are good.

What can I use it for?

This is a very strong tool for working on improving your business' ability to keep customers you have already acquired or just plain and simple getting more return business.

The first thing you can do is to directly approach the people who left your business.

Do it yourself

My Customer Churn Rate is:

I rate my CCR as:

This is what I will do to improve my CCR:

Customer Lifetime Period

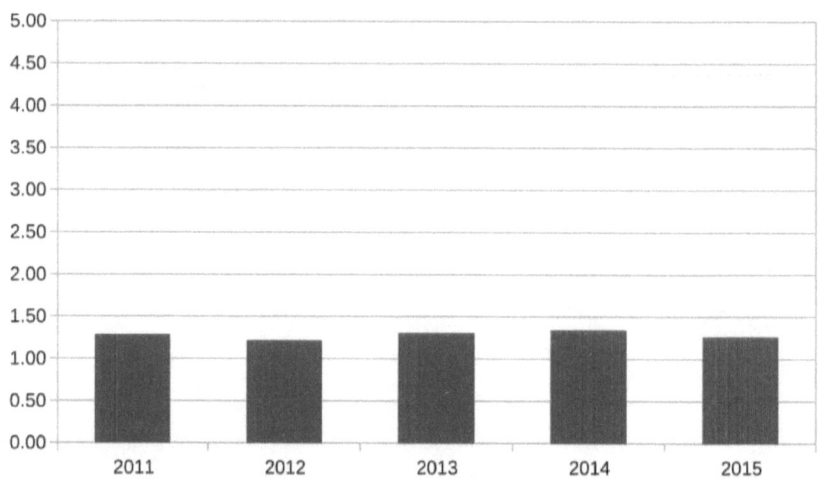

What is this?

The Customer Lifetime Period shows you the average number of years a customer remains in your business.

Subjective notes on the example: "This is a very low Lifetime Period as it more or less means all customers are gone after little more than a year. The first investigation could look into the reason why customers are leaving."

How do I find it?

This is just the reciprocal of the Customer Churn Rate: 100% / Customer Churn Rate (per year) = Customer Lifetime Period in years.

How easy is it?

Once you have the Customer Churn Rate it is very easy.

What is good?

Higher values are good.

What can I use it for?

This is tightly connected to Retention and Churn Rate but shows you how long or short a period your customers are in your business for so it mainly illustrates exactly how good (or bad) you are at keeping your customers.

Business Intelligence

Do it yourself

My CLP is:

I rate my CLP as:

This is what I will do to improve my CLP:

Participants Registered

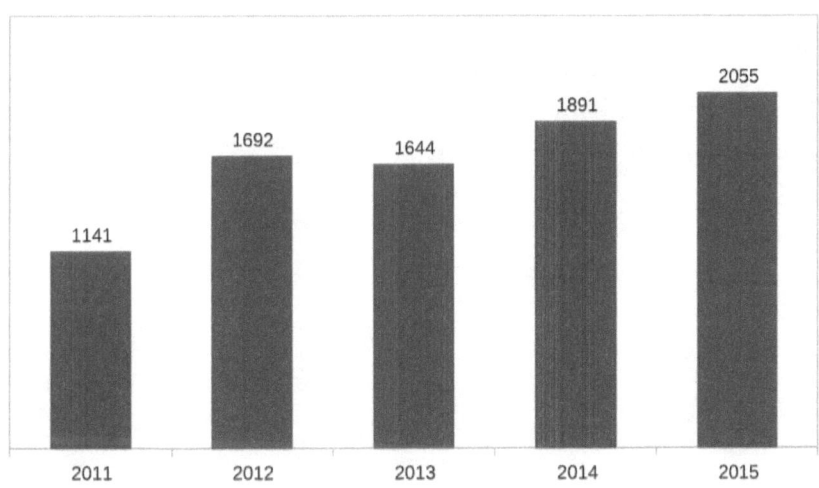

What is this?

The number of participants registered at year end. Waiting list is not included.

Subjective notes: "In parallel to the extremely low Retention Rate this growth is massive and should be investigated further to gather information on why and how the company can attract new customers whilst not being able to hold on to them.

How do I find it?

Just count your paying/registered customers at year end. You can do the same for your waiting lists if you have such.

How easy is it?

Easy

What is good?

Higher values are good.

What can I use it for?

This can be used as a stepping stone for looking deeper into figures like how efficiently you utilize resources.

Do it yourself

My total number of participants is:

I rate my number as:

This is what I will do to improve my total number of participants:

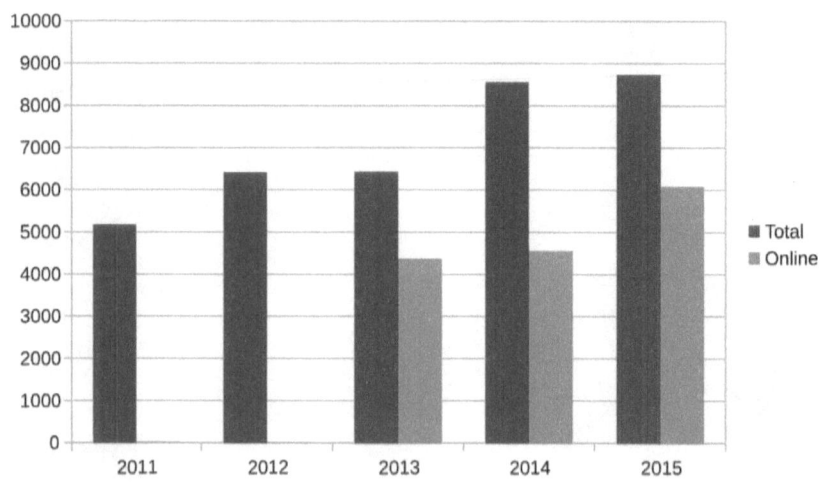

What is this?

The total number of registrations compared to on-line bookings as part of total.

Subjective notes: "On-line booking was introduced in 2013 and is a fast growing part of the on-boarding procedure."

How do I find it?

You find the numbers in your database and/or in your on-line booking system.

If you have the numbers you can even split the on-line registrations into

How easy is it?

If you have the numbers in your database it is easy.

What is good?

N/A (Even though the more registrations in total the better.)

What can I use it for?

This can basically be split into all the different channels you use for registering customers and you use the numbers to target your marketing and on-boarding resources where they make the biggest impact.

Consider splitting the on-line registrations further into areas of technology like mobile compared to PC/laptop, browser type, traffic source and the like in order to pinpoint the best markets.

Business Intelligence

Do it yourself

My Registration Type numbers are:

My most important Registration Type is:

I rate this as:

This is what I will do to improve my most important Registration Type:

Business Revenue

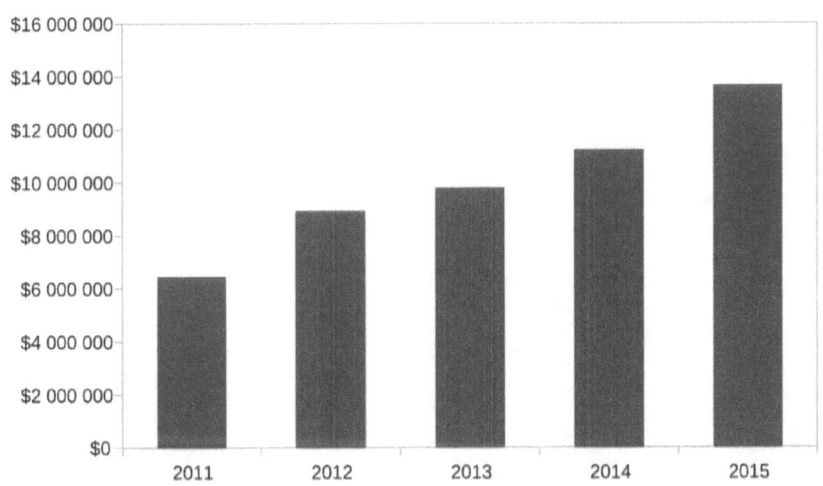

What is this?

Total revenue for all classes running the given year.

Subjective notes: "Further investigate how this substantial growth rate is maintained and whether or not the same growth rate is applicable to the bottom line."

How do I find it?

You find this in your book keeping.

How easy is it?

Easy.

What is good?

Higher values are good.

What can I use it for?

To see whether or not you are making money and how much.

Business Intelligence

Do it yourself

My Business Revenue is:

I rate my BR as:

This is what I will do to improve my revenue:

Group Revenue Rate

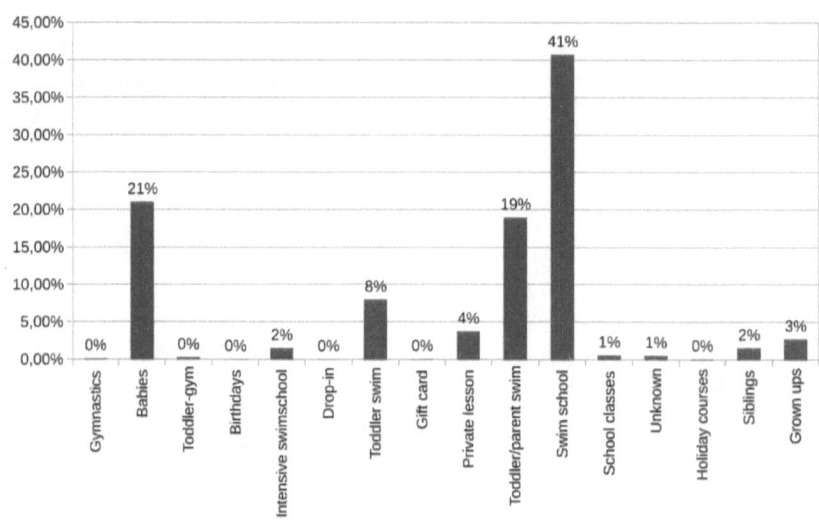

What is this?

Total revenue for 2015 split into groups/business areas.

Subjective notes: "Noticeable that only three groups account for 81% of the total revenue.
Objectively consider closing some of the activities in groups with extremely low revenue rates."

How do I find it?

You should be able to read this from your CRM system.

How easy is it?

Easy if your CRM shows it. Very hard if it does not.

What is good?

N/A

What can I use it for?

You can use the numbers to see where your business is most profitable and next to see where you might be able to save or allocate resources.

Business Intelligence

Do it yourself

My Group Revenue Rates are:

My most important groups are:

My least important groups are:

I rate my GRR as:

This is what I will do to improve my GRR:

Business Intelligence

About the author

"Johan Faerch has his roots in the Danish Army Special Operations Forces 'The Jaegercorps' honored with the US Presidential Unit Citation. The skill sets for executing special operations take immense amounts of data to master. Fast forward to the present Johan now helps businesses making sense of their data and with how to put the same data to work. Data utilized the right way can be the difference between success and failure for a company which is why more and more executives are focusing on this area. His mission is to enable man to keep up with the machine!"

www.ingramcontent.com/pod-product-compliance
Lightning Source LLC
Chambersburg PA
CBHW031504210526
45463CB00003B/1072